ANNE **FRANK**

Holocaust Diarist

BY ALEXIS BURLING

CONTENT CONSULTANT
ARNOLD KRAMMER, PHD
PROFESSOR EMERITUS OF HISTORY
TEXAS A&M UNIVERSITY

Essential Library

An Imprint of Abdo Publishing | abdopublishing.com

abdopublishing.com

Published by Abdo Publishing, a division of ABDO, PO Box 398166, Minneapolis, Minnesota 55439.

Printed in the United States of America, North Mankato, Minnesota
022016
092016

THIS BOOK CONTAINS RECYCLED MATERIALS

Cover Photo: DPA/Corbis
Interior Photos: Photo collection of the Anne Frank House, Amsterdam, 4, 13, 44, 61; Massimo Catarinella/iStockphoto, 7; Fine Art Images/SuperStock, 11, 14, 23, 48; Charles Russell Collection, NARA, 18; Berliner Verlag/Archiv/Picture-Alliance/DPA/AP Images, 25; DPA/Corbis, 26, 36; Bildarchiv Pisarek/akg-images/Newscom, 29; AP Images, 33; Leo La Valle/EPA/Newscom, 39; Piero Oliosi/Polaris, 43; Michael Teller/akg-images/Newscom, 46; Glasshouse Images/Newscom, 54; World History Archive/Newscom, 58; akg-images/Newscom, 63, 91; Anne Frank Fonds Basel/DPA/Corbis, 64; Public Domain, 69; Reproduction/EPA/Corbis, 72; Hulton-Deutsch Collection/Corbis, 75; US Army, 76; Aff/Afs/Sunshine/ZumaPress/Newscom, 81; Ullstein Bild/Getty Images, 83; Anne Frank Fonds Basel/Getty Images, 85; REX/Newscom, 86; Hans Engbers/Shutterstock Images, 95

Editor: Jon Westmark
Series Designer: Becky Daum

Cataloging-in-Publication Data

Names: Burling, Alexis, author.
Title: Anne Frank: Holocaust diarist / by Alexis Burling.
Description: Minneapolis, MN : Abdo Publishing, [2017] | Series: Essential lives | Includes bibliographical references and index.
Identifiers: LCCN 2015959871 | ISBN 9781680782981 (lib. bdg.) | ISBN 9781680774788 (ebook)
Subjects: LCSH: Frank, Anne, 1929-1945--Juvenile literature. | Jews--Netherlands--Amsterdam--Biography--Juvenile literature. | Jewish children in the Holocaust--Netherlands--Amsterdam--Biography--Juvenile literature. | Holocaust, Jewish (1939-1945)--Netherlands--Amsterdam--Juvenile literature. | Amsterdam (Netherlands)--Biography--Juvenile literature.
Classification: DDC 940.53/18092 [B]--dc23
LC record available at http://lccn.loc.gov/2015959871

CONTENTS

CHAPTER ONE

BETRAYED

It was the beginning of August 1944, and World War II (1939–1945) had been raging across Europe for nearly five years. Adolf Hitler, the leader of Germany and its Nazi Party, was fighting to maintain control of the continent. Millions of soldiers had died in gruesome battles on the ground, in the air, and at sea. Many millions more Jews, Roma (Gypsies), Jehovah's Witnesses, communists, homosexuals, and others were being arrested and systematically slaughtered in Nazi-controlled concentration camps scattered throughout Germany, Poland, and the surrounding areas. The Nazis believed these groups of people were inferior to the Aryan race and wanted to exterminate them.

Thus far, 15-year-old Anne Frank and her parents, Otto and Edith; sister, Margot; family friends Hermann and Auguste van Pels and their 17-year-old son, Peter; and dentist Fritz Pfeffer—all Jewish—had eluded capture. They were hiding in what they called the Secret

Anne Frank, *second from right,* and her family hid from Nazi oppression during World War II.

ARYAN

In ancient times, *Aryan* was the name given to a group of light-skinned people who settled in Iran and northern India. In 1850, a different definition of the word was made popular by French writer and diplomat Joseph-Arthur, comte de Gobineau. Gobineau defined Aryans as a race of light-skinned Nordic people who were believed to be racially superior to their dark-skinned counterparts. Hitler and the Nazis used this notion of racial superiority as their basis for attempting to exterminate all Jews, Roma, and other non-Aryans during World War II.

Annex, a cramped series of rooms hidden behind a bookcase on the third floor of a four-story row house neighboring the Prinsengracht canal in Amsterdam, the Netherlands.

For two years, the Franks and their friends had been separated from the outside world. They remained inside at all times, stayed away from windows, and kept noise levels to a minimum. Despite the dreadful circumstances, they tried to make the best of their situation, spending their days reading, writing, cooking, or playing cards. Meanwhile, Otto Frank's Christian business partners, Johannes Kleiman and Victor Kugler, kept Otto's spice and pectin company, Opekta, running on the ground floor. But the morning of August 4 was different. An anonymous caller had tipped off the Sicherheitsdienst (SD), the intelligence arm of the Nazi

The row house in which the Secret Annex is located

Party, about the Secret Annex's existence. The Franks' luck was about to run out.

Captured

Anne woke up at approximately 8:00 a.m., just as the sun began streaming through the leaves of the chestnut tree outside the window. She planned to catch up on journaling that morning. It had been three days since

ANONYMOUS INFORMANT

On the morning of August 4, 1944, an anonymous informant tipped off the gestapo, or Nazi police, about the existence of the Secret Annex, leading to the arrest of Anne, her family, and her friends.

In 1948, Johannes Kleiman asked the POD, the Dutch equivalent to the Federal Bureau of Investigation (FBI), to find out the informant's identity. The investigation centered on Willem van Maaren, who worked in Opekta's warehouse. But the POD did not uncover any conclusive evidence about who the betrayer actually was. In 1963, another case was launched, again focusing on van Maaren and his possible motives. Investigators tracked down Karl Silberbauer, the SD officer in charge of the arrest. They questioned him about what happened the morning the Franks were arrested, but the interview did not yield any new information about the anonymous informant's identity. The case hit a dead end and closed.

By 1975, many of the people involved in the Secret Annex raid had died, including Julius Dettman, the SD officer who took the call from the informant, and van Maaren. Although two other suspects have been put forward—Lena Hartog-van Bladeren, the wife of a stockroom employee, and Tonny Ahlers, a colleague of Otto's—the truth about the identity of the traitor remains a mystery to this day.

she had written anything in her diary. But first, she needed to finalize the grocery list to give to Miep Gies, one of the four Opekta employees who knew about the Annex and snuck in food and supplies. Little did Anne know that the shopping planned for that day would never get done.

At approximately 11:30 a.m., a Dutch man barged into 263 Prinsengracht without knocking. He held a gun in his hand and pointed it at Gies and two of her coworkers, Kleiman and Bep Voskuijl. The armed man yelled, "Stay put! Don't move!" Minutes later, an olive-green truck pulled up in front of the building. A group of Dutch policemen and a German SD officer, Karl Silberbauer, jumped out and demanded to be given a tour of the house. Gies refused but was forced to hand over her keys.

KARL SILBERBAUER

After World War II ended and Anne Frank's diary became popular, rumors began circulating that it might be fake. In order to refute this theory, Simon Wiesenthal, an investigator known for tracking down Nazis, started searching for Karl Silberbauer, the gestapo officer who arrested the inhabitants of the Secret Annex.

In 1963, Wiesenthal located Silberbauer in Vienna, Austria, where he was a member of the police force. Silberbauer was not convicted of any crimes once he was found, but the fact of his existence helped prove that Anne's diary was authentic.

"Aren't you ashamed that you are helping Jewish garbage?" the SD officer spat at Gies as he stalked off to join the police in searching the upper floors. "I'll be back to check on you. One wrong move and off you go to prison too," he said.[1]

The minutes ticked by as two grueling hours passed. Suddenly, Gies heard something she had hoped she would never be forced to hear: the sound of furniture being thrown about followed by footfalls in the stairwell that led up to the hideaway. The police had discovered her friends' hiding place. "I could tell from their footsteps that they were coming down like beaten dogs," she wrote later in her autobiography.[2] Before Gies had a chance to say good-bye, her friends—along with Kleiman and Kugler, who had been listening in another room—were taken away.

GERMAN PLUNDER

When the gestapo went door to door arresting Jews and hauling them away to concentration camps, important valuables were often left behind. Expensive artwork, typewriters, radios, jewelry, fur coats, and safes full of money, were all up for grabs. Hitler decreed that anything left behind by the Jews would be rounded up and redistributed to members of the Nazi Party and to German citizens.

A Legacy Revealed

Hours later, after they were sure the police would not return,

Anne's plaid diary

Gies, her husband, and Voskuijl crept upstairs to assess how much damage had been done. What they found was distressing. The Franks' cashbox was missing, and furniture had been smashed and splintered. Tattered clothing had been ripped from dresser drawers and flung about in heaps. Shattered dishes lined the kitchen floor. It looked as though a tornado had hit and left a mess in its wake.

But in Otto and Edith Frank's bedroom, something caught Gies's attention. There on the rug was Anne's red-and-tan checkered journal and some other notebooks. Next to them was a pile of papers containing Anne's delicate handwriting—remnants of notes from her treasured diaries. Without thinking twice, Gies scooped up all of the writings, hugging them to her chest.

"I will keep everything," she said. "I'll keep everything safe for Anne until she comes back."[3]

But Anne would never return to her Amsterdam home. Aside from her father, neither would the rest of the Frank family. Along with millions of other men, women, and children considered undesirable by the Nazis, the Franks would be stripped of their belongings, packed into trains, and shipped off to concentration camps.

By the time World War II ended in the summer of 1945, more than 50 million people had been killed.[4] Entire ancestral lines were wiped out. Most of the people in concentration camps perished from starvation, endless work, or ruthless execution. But Otto Frank survived. In January 1945, Auschwitz—the concentration camp where Otto was being held—was

Miep Gies, *left*, was hired by Otto Frank, *right*, in 1933. She worked for the pectin company throughout the war.

liberated. With Hitler's army on the verge of defeat, Otto began the long journey back to the building he once called home, in order to grieve the loss of his loved ones.

Five months after Otto arrived in Amsterdam, he officially returned to work at his former company. After discovering that Gies had tucked away Anne's journals in a desk drawer for safekeeping, Otto made a solemn promise to share his daughter's writings with the world. He painstakingly edited them and created what he hoped would be a publishable book. In honor of his daughter and the more than 6 million Jews murdered during the Holocaust, the diary delivered a deeply distressing yet true-to-life view of one of the most harrowing periods in history. The story of Anne's life needed to be heard.

CHAPTER TWO

A TUMULTUOUS CHILDHOOD

Annelies Marie Frank was born on June 12, 1929. For the first four years of her life, she and her older sister, Margot, lived with their parents in an upper-middle-class neighborhood in Frankfurt am Main, Germany. After serving as a lieutenant in the German army during World War I (1914–1918), Anne's father, Otto, inherited and ran his family's bank. Anne's mother, Edith, a member of the prestigious Holländer family, stayed home and took care of the children.

Until the late 1920s, Otto and Edith Frank had lived relatively carefree and comfortable lives. Both from wealthy Jewish families, the couple enjoyed exploring the cultural activities they adored as children. Otto relished going to the opera and listening to cello music, while Edith found comfort in attending synagogue and vacationing on the German coast.

Anne, *front*, and Margot, *left*, often called their father Pim.

But in the early 1930s, life as the Franks knew it began to change. When the US stock market crashed in 1929, countries all over the world were affected. Germany was one of the hardest hit. Much of the country's financial infrastructure had been built on credit and foreign loans following its defeat during World War I. When other countries could no longer afford to lend money and resources to Germany, its economy failed. Six million German workers lost their jobs, and unemployment levels rose. The price of food and oil skyrocketed, and supplies became scarce. Many

DADDY'S GIRL

Though Edith Frank often spent time with her daughters while their father was at work, Anne did not have a particularly warm relationship with her mother. Instead, Anne much preferred her father's company, especially the time they spent reading together or cracking jokes.

Anne's dislike for her mother was so strong during her teenage years that she often complained about her mother in her diary. A typical entry: "Yesterday Mother and I had another run-in and she really kicked up a fuss. She told Daddy all of my sins and started to cry, which made me cry too, and I already had such an awful headache. I finally told Daddy that I love 'him' more than I do Mother, to which he replied that it was just a passing phase, but I don't think so. I simply can't stand Mother, and I have to force myself not to snap at her all the time, and to stay calm, when I'd rather slap her across the face."[1] It was only when Anne and her mother were thrown together in the concentration camps years later that Anne realized how much she loved her mother.

banks, including Otto's, were forced to close.

Consequently, Germany's Reichstag, or parliament, was thrust into a period of transition. The German people desperately needed a solution to their nation's problems. They were determined to root out those responsible for the country's mounting shortages, and they longed for a new leader who could solve the economic crisis and lift them out of poverty.

That leader was Adolf Hitler. When Hitler became chancellor on January 30, 1933, many Germans felt hopeful and empowered by the passionate orator's speeches, which promised new jobs and a resurgent, all-powerful German government. Hitler's party, the National Socialist German Workers' Party,

THE TREATY OF VERSAILLES

On November 11, 1918, World War I officially ended. Germany was on the losing side. As punishment, German leaders were ordered to sign the Treaty of Versailles on June 28, 1919. The treaty contained a long list of terms Germany was forced to accept. Germany had to give up all of its overseas territories and redistribute much of its gained land. Germany's army was cut back to 100,000 men, and German use of submarines and tanks was prohibited.

Germany also had to admit full responsibility for the war. The German government was forced to pay heavy fines to other countries until the Great Depression led to the cancellation of repayment reparations in 1932. Many historians view the Treaty of Versailles' harsh terms as a catalyst for Hitler's rise to power.

Adolf Hitler quickly gained influence by promising to bring Germany back to greatness.

or Nazi Party, proudly championed the comeback of the common citizen. And more important, Hitler provided Germans with a familiar scapegoat that could be blamed for the nation's economic downturn: the Jews.

From Frankfurt to Amsterdam

Similar to many Jewish families in 1933, the Franks had fallen on hard times. After Otto's bank collapsed, he needed to go elsewhere to find work so he could support his family. Erich Elias, Otto's brother-in-law and banking partner until 1929, put Otto in touch with the managers of Opekta, the Swiss pectin company where Elias now worked. Opekta's managers were searching for someone to open an office in Amsterdam and thought Otto would be a perfect candidate for the position.

MEIN KAMPF

Hitler's *Mein Kampf*, which means "My Struggle" in German, was published in two volumes in 1925 and 1927. In it, Hitler describes his childhood and experiences during World War I. He also outlines his social beliefs, mainly his perception of Aryans as a so-called genius race and Jews as inferior. According to Hitler, "the sacred mission of the German people [was] to assemble and preserve the most valuable racial elements . . . and raise them to the dominant position."[2] Though Hitler was not the first leader to promote anti-Semitic beliefs, *Mein Kampf* became a foundational document of the Nazi Party and an impetus for the Holocaust.

Otto was looking to emigrate from Germany for other reasons, as well. Since Hitler's rise to power, the German government had placed more and more restrictions on Jews. Germans boycotted Jewish-owned businesses. Jewish children were segregated from other children in schools. And on April 7, 1933, the Law for the Restoration of the Professional Civil Service was passed, which prohibited Jews from participating in civil or government professions. Consequently, hundreds of Jewish teachers, judges, and government workers were dismissed from their jobs. Not long after, Jewish musicians, artists, and philosophers were also dismissed. It was no longer safe or wise for the Franks to stay in Germany.

BOOK BURNING

In 1933, the Nazi Minister for Public Enlightenment and Propaganda, Joseph Goebbels, issued an edict to purge German cultural institutions of any literature, music, or teachings that possessed an "un-German spirit" and went against Hitler's political agenda. In solidarity on May 10, pro-Nazi university students across Germany burned more than 25,000 volumes of "un-German" books, including works by German-born writers Bertolt Brecht, Thomas Mann, and Karl Marx, and American authors Ernest Hemingway and Helen Keller.

In the summer of 1933, Otto hurriedly journeyed to Amsterdam to research his business options. He formed an independent branch of Opekta, the Swiss pectin production company, using a loan from his brother-in-law. The company became firmly established in September, and Edith joined her husband in Amsterdam. Anne and Margot stayed with Edith's mother in Germany until Otto and Edith were settled in Amsterdam. Margot made the journey to Amsterdam in December, accompanied by Edith's brothers, Julius and Walter Holländer. Four-year-old Anne followed on February 16, 1934, Margot's eighth birthday.

A Temporary Reprieve

The Franks' first few years in Amsterdam were pleasant—a welcome change from their life in Germany. They lived in a three-bedroom apartment on the third floor of a sand-colored brick apartment building. The apartment was not as spacious as their home in Frankfurt, but it provided the family with the security they needed. Plus, they were surrounded by open-minded and religiously tolerant neighbors, many of whom were Jewish immigrants from Germany who enjoyed having friends over to discuss politics or theater.

"Although these people had not all known each other beforehand, they had much in common," remembered Miep Santrouschitz, a Dutch friend who became Miep Gies through marriage in 1941. "Mr. Frank liked the idea of introducing these refugees to Dutch people who were interested in their lot, in why they had fled, and in their welfare here in Holland."[3]

Otto's business was expanding, too. He hired Victor Kugler and Santrouschitz to help run his company's daily affairs. Opekta did so well under their joint leadership that it grew to incorporate a spice-selling arm called Pectacon with the help of butcher Hermann van Pels. Johannes Kleiman joined the staff in 1938 as Opekta and Pectacon's accountant. He had previously worked in the Amsterdam branch of Otto's bank, and the two had rekindled their friendship when Otto moved to the city.

While their father was busy at work, the Frank sisters were busy with social engagements and schoolwork. Margot was more quiet and studious, always with a book nearby. She pleased her parents by consistently getting top marks on her report cards. Anne did well in writing and drawing, but she never excelled in math. Instead, she preferred to play hopscotch with her friends Hanneli Goslar and Sanne Ledermann during recess. She also got in trouble for being rebellious and talking too much during class.

"In the Netherlands, after those experiences in Germany, it was as if our life was restored to us," Otto recalled, looking back on that time many years later.

Margot studied hard in school and hoped to become a nurse.

"In those days it was possible for us to start over and to feel free."[4]

DACHAU

On March 22, 1933, Germany established its first concentration camp to house political prisoners and enemies of the state. Located outside the town of Munich, Germany, the camp, called Dachau, housed more than 188,000 prisoners between 1933 and 1945, including more than 28,000 who died during its final six years of operation. It was the only camp that remained open during the entire Nazi regime.

But that feeling of freedom was short-lived. On August 19, 1934, Hitler dissolved the German presidency and declared himself führer, or leader, of the German people—an action that effectively placed him above the laws of the state. On September 15, 1935, he enacted a series of anti-Semitic laws that were designed to punish Jews and, later, all non-Aryan people. Under the Nuremberg Laws, Jews were defined not by their religious beliefs, but by their ancestral heritage. Therefore, any person who had three or four Jewish grandparents was considered Jewish, regardless of whether that person identified as a Jew, belonged to a Jewish religious community, or converted to a different religion. Furthermore, all Jews were seen as noncitizens and were forbidden to marry anyone of German origin.

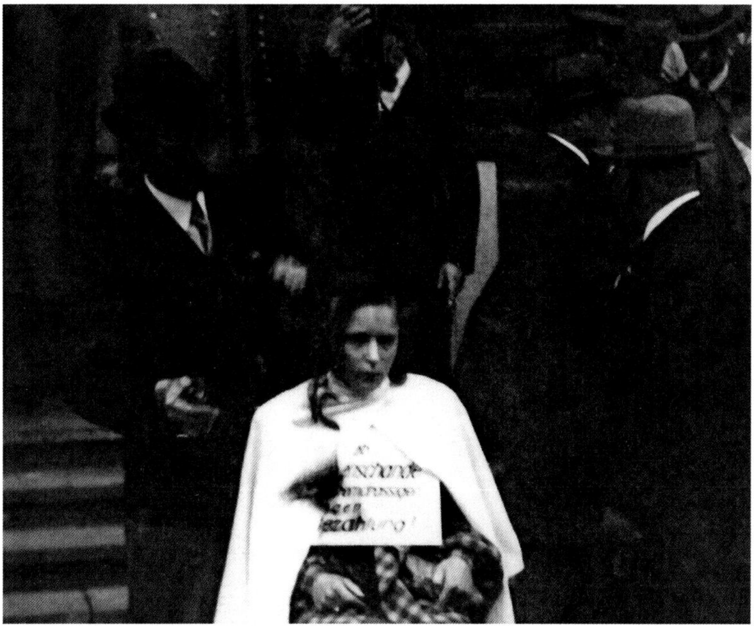

Under the Nuremberg Laws, German women who married Jewish men could be shamed publicly by having their hair cut off.

Offenders who broke any of the rules were considered criminals and could be punished by law.

Soon, Nazi beliefs began spreading beyond Germany's borders into neighboring countries. As a result, the restrictions and religious intolerance that had plagued the Franks in Germany became commonplace in Amsterdam. By 1938, the outlook for the city's Jewish population looked grim. But the Franks could not have known how much worse circumstances were about to get—for them and for other non-Aryans around the world.

CHAPTER THREE

THE SEEDS OF THE HOLOCAUST

Since the time of Jesus's crucifixion, when many Christians believed Jews were responsible for his death, anti-Semitic beliefs were not uncommon in Europe. Over time, anti-Semitism worked its way into common thought. Laws and policies even enforced discrimination against Jews. In the Middle Ages, Jews were denied citizenship or expelled from their countries. By the 1800s, Jews were commonly considered inferior because of their race and religious beliefs. Jews became a scapegoat for society's political and social problems. Following World War I and throughout the 1930s, when economies across the world crashed, it was easy for the seeds of anti-Semitism to be replanted once again by Hitler. His Nazi Party promised change by eradicating the supposed culprit: the Jews. After Hitler's rise to power in 1933, nearly one in four Jews—approximately 150,000 people—immigrated

Anne, *right,* was three, and Margot, *left,* was six when Hitler became Germany's chancellor on January 30, 1933.

THE CAUSE OF KRISTALLNACHT

Kristallnacht was not only an aggressive step in the Nazis' plan to exterminate the Jews; it was also an act of retaliation. In 1938, Hitler expelled thousands of Polish-born Jews from Germany, including the parents of 17-year-old Herschel Grynszpan, who had resided in the country since 1911. At first, his family, along with many others, was not accepted into Poland and was forced to stay in a refugee camp on the Germany-Poland border.

To avenge his parents' plight, Herschel, who was living illegally in Paris, France, entered the German embassy there on November 7, 1938, and shot and killed Ernst vom Rath, a German diplomat. The German government responded by unleashing Kristallnacht on the Jews.

to more tolerant countries to escape persecution.[1] But for Jews who stayed in Germany, the restrictions on their liberties and the abuse they faced each day only increased.

On July 6, 1938, 32 leaders from around the world met in Évian-les-Baines, France, for a conference. They hoped to come up with a solution for how to help German Jews. But in the end, most countries, including the United States, were not willing to accept more immigrants—even persecuted Jewish ones.

Then, on November 9, 1938, an incident occurred that became a crucial turning point in the fate of the Jewish people. It was called Kristallnacht, "Night of Broken Glass," and it was a terrifying foreshadowing of events to come. The Nazi

Kristallnacht was meant to appear like spontaneous violence, but Nazi troops had clear orders to burn synagogues and destroy Jewish businesses.

government's Minister for Public Enlightenment and Propaganda, Joseph Goebbels, organized the incident. Overnight, more than 7,500 Jewish-owned businesses, synagogues, community centers, and homes throughout Germany were burned or looted by Nazi troops, the Hitler Youth, and Nazi sympathizers. Ninety-one Jewish people were killed.[2] The next morning, nearly 30,000 Jewish men were arrested and sent to concentration camps, including Dachau and Buchenwald, where many of them died from starvation and brutal work conditions.[3]

Such pogroms, or violent acts of racial discrimination, had not yet reached Amsterdam, where the Franks and their Jewish neighbors listened to the stories about what was taking place in Germany. Otto and Edith were appalled to hear their German friends' businesses had been destroyed. Margot and Anne could not believe their old playmates were no longer allowed to watch films in movie theaters and were expelled from

KINDERTRANSPORT

In the late 1930s, people around the world were horrified by what was happening to German Jews, in particular the events that had taken place during Kristallnacht. Foreign governments wanted to help.

In 1938, spurred on by refugee aid groups, the British government organized and implemented the Kindertransport, "Children's Transport." Beginning on December 1 and continuing over the next two years, nearly 10,000 unaccompanied refugees under the age of 17 from Germany and German-occupied territories, such as Austria and the Czech Republic, were permitted to travel to the United Kingdom using temporary travel documents. Approximately 7,500 of the children were Jewish.

The rules of the program were strict. Each child was allowed one small suitcase and had to be sponsored by a British citizen or official organization. The children were then expected to return to their home countries once the war was over.

The last known transport took place on May 14, 1940, when the Dutch surrendered to Germany. By that time, fighting had begun raging on land and at sea, and it was too dangerous for the program to continue during wartime conditions. After World War II ended, many of the Kindertransport children whose parents had been killed during the Holocaust immigrated to Israel, the United States, and Australia rather than returning to Germany.

German schools. The Franks hoped against their better judgment that it was merely a problem in Germany and that they would continue to be safe as long as they stayed in the Netherlands.

War Breaks Out

From 1938 and into the next year, the power of Hitler's Nazi Party continued to grow unchecked. On January 30, 1939, the führer gave a speech to the German parliament. In it, Hitler said Jews were officially responsible for the financial crisis that had crippled the world's economies. He promised the "annihilation of the Jewish race in Europe" and said if that meant murdering what he considered to be subhuman people by the hundreds of thousands, so be it.[4] The Holocaust had begun.

AXIS VS. ALLIES

The two opposing sides during World War II were the Axis and Allied powers. The major countries in the Axis alliance were Germany, Japan, and Italy. The United States, the United Kingdom, France, the Soviet Union, and China formed the Allied force, which eventually won the war.

Hitler was also now more determined than ever to expand his sphere of influence and to bring other countries under his control. He had already taken control of Austria in 1938 and Czechoslovakia in early

1939, but Hitler wanted to push Germany's borders farther. On September 1, 1939, he invaded Poland. The aggressive action prompted the United Kingdom and France to declare war on Germany on September 3. Just two decades after the world had been embroiled in a conflict that caused the deaths of more than 37 million people, World War II began.[5]

Within a month of Hitler's invasion of Poland, the country's capital, Warsaw, surrendered, and the western half of the country fell under German control. Just as in Germany, strict regulations were put into place over the next year. Jews and other "undesirables" were deported from Germany to Poland.

Still, Hitler hungered for more territory. By 1940, the Nazis had invaded Norway and Denmark. Belgium, Luxembourg, and northern France fell under Hitler's control, too. In April 1940, construction began in Poland on Auschwitz, the Nazis' largest concentration camp. The camp's

WARSAW GHETTO

Nearly 400,000 Polish and imported German Jews were placed into a 1.3-square-mile (3.4 sq. km) area in Warsaw, called a ghetto. The area was cut off from the rest of the city by a wall ten feet (3 m) tall.[6] Space was tight in the ghetto, and the residents were forced to wear white armbands emblazoned with a blue Star of David, a symbol used to identify them as Jewish.

The wall around the Warsaw ghetto closed off hundreds of streets and streetcar lines.

purpose was to house enemies of the Nazi regime and eradicate Jews.

The Franks feared the relatively free existence they enjoyed in Amsterdam would soon come to an end. Then, on May 10, 1940, the Franks' fears were realized—the German military began to bomb the Netherlands. Four days later, the country surrendered.

THE FINAL SOLUTION

On January 20, 1942, high-ranking members of the Nazi military organized the Wannsee Conference to discuss the implementation of what Hitler called the Final Solution, a plan for the systematic murder of Jews throughout Europe. Initially, the Nazis planned to exterminate 11 million Jews in Germany, Poland, the Soviet Union, and nonoccupied countries, such as Ireland, Turkey, and the United Kingdom.

Between 1941 and 1944, 6 million Jews were gassed, shot, or executed in six concentration camps set up specifically to carry out the Final Solution: Auschwitz, Birkenau, Belzec, Chelmno, Majdanek, Sobibor, and Treblinka.

Amsterdam Occupied

From 1940 to 1942, the restraints that had been placed on the Franks' Jewish friends in Germany were implemented and strictly enforced throughout Amsterdam. No Jews were allowed on streetcars or on bicycles. Jews were permitted to shop only between 3:00 p.m. and 5:00 p.m., and they were forced to be indoors by

6:00 p.m. Movie theaters, swimming pools, dance halls, and nonsegregated schools were off-limits. Jews were also forced to wear yellow patches shaped like the Star of David on the outside of their clothes at all times.

"After May 1940, the good times were few and far between," Anne wrote. "First there was the war, then the capitulation, and then the arrival of the Germans, which is when the trouble started for the Jews."[7]

Yet despite the increased restrictions placed on Jews, Anne did her best to live the life of a normal teenager. She enjoyed sunbathing on the beach, until Dutch Jews were banned from beaches in July 1941. Anne also enjoyed reading books on the roof of her family's apartment building.

To protect Opekta and Pectacon, Otto signed over the directorship of his company to his Christian business partner, Kugler. Kleiman helped manage daily affairs. As an additional precaution, the joint company would now be officially called Gies & Co., after his longtime friend and colleague Miep and her new husband, Jan.

At the time, Otto believed he could save his company if he just made a few changes. But could he do the same for his family?

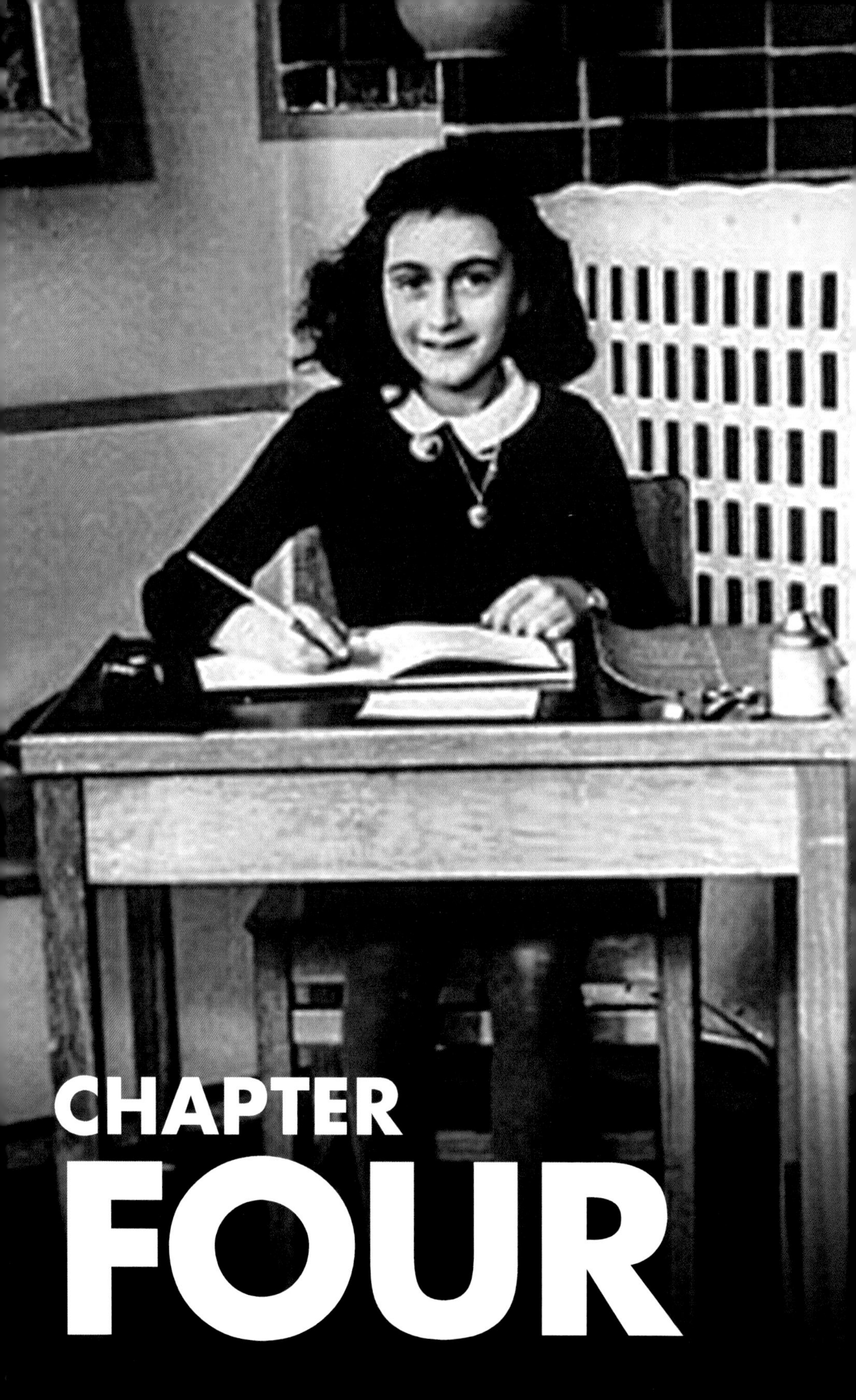

CHAPTER FOUR

A YEAR OF CHANGE

On the morning of June 12, 1942, Anne woke up in a flurry of excitement. It was her thirteenth birthday, and she had finally become a teenager—a thrilling change that meant greater independence both at school and at home. Plenty of unhappy changes had taken place around Anne over the past year—anti-Jewish laws had made her transfer schools to the Jewish Lyceum in September 1941, her grandmother had died in January, and her beloved bike had been stolen in May. But Anne was determined to make her birthday weekend a happy one.

She planned a giant celebration and invited all her friends. Hanneli and Sanne came, as well as another new friend from school, Jacqueline van Maarsen. Hello Silverberg, a handsome boy who had taken an interest in Anne, was also invited. Edith baked a strawberry tart, and the kids crowded around the living room film

Anne enjoyed her time at the Sixth Montessori School, which she attended until September 1941.

JACQUELINE VAN MAARSEN

Jacqueline van Maarsen was one of Anne's best friends. Her father was Jewish, but she was saved from the terrors most German-born Jews were forced to endure. In Judaism, Jewish identity is passed down through the mother. But Jacqueline's mother was not Jewish; she converted when she married Jacqueline's father. Under the Nuremberg Race Laws of 1935, anyone who had three or four Jewish grandparents was declared Jewish. Jacqueline had only two. When Jacqueline's mother went to the Nazi authorities and informed them of her heritage, they removed her family's name from the deportation list. Jacqueline's family was saved—including her Jewish father—and survived the Holocaust.

projector to watch *The Lighthouse Keeper*, a movie starring Anne's favorite celebrity dog, Rin Tin Tin.

Otto and Edith tried their best to act as though there was not a war going on. Consequently, the party was a huge success, with many presents. Anne adored her new blue blouse, as well as the lovely brooch, the bouquet of roses, and the puzzle she was given. A book she received, *Dutch Sagas and Legends* by Joseph Khozn, was special too. But the gift she cherished most was from her father: a red-and-tan checkered diary in which she could write her deepest, most secret thoughts.

Later that evening, Anne wrote the first entry in the journal, which she decided to call Kitty. "I hope I will be able to confide everything to you, as I have never been

Anne was not surprised when she received the checkered diary. She had picked it out days before her birthday.

able to confide in anyone," she wrote. "I hope you will be a great source of comfort and support."[1]

Otto's Plan

For the next few weeks, Anne tried to ignore news of the war and maintain her cheerful attitude by keeping herself busy. She spent luxurious afternoons taking long strolls and talking about everything under the sun with Hello. She edited and revised parts of a fairy tale she was working on called "Eva's Dream." And she wrote as much as she could in her diary.

"Writing in a diary is a really strange experience for someone like me," Anne wrote on June 20. "Not only because I've never written anything before, but because it seems to me that later on neither I nor anyone else will be interested in the musings of a 13-year-old school girl. Oh well, it doesn't matter . . . Paper has more patience than people."[2]

One day in early July, Otto took Anne for a walk around Merwedeplein, the triangle of buildings near the Franks' home. He explained that he and Edith were putting together a secret plan for the family to go into hiding. Jews were easy to locate because they were required to carry identity papers, and over the previous six months, thousands of Jews had been rounded up across Amsterdam and sent in cattle cars to concentration camps. In order for the Franks to get through the war alive, Otto insisted, they needed to disappear before they could be captured.

Anne had many questions. Where would they go? Somewhere in Amsterdam? To the beach, where the Franks sometimes vacationed during the summer? What would they do with all of their furniture, their belongings? How long would they be hidden? Otto refused to answer Anne's questions but assured her she would find out soon enough.

The Turning Point

Otto hoped to wait a few weeks before carrying out his plan. But a knock at the Franks' door on July 5 signaled the family needed to disappear much sooner. A letter had arrived in the form of a call-up notice. One of 1,000 Jews who received notices that day, 16-year-old Margot had been ordered to report to the Gestapo Central Office in nine days' time. If she failed to comply, she would be arrested.

FEBRUARY 22, 1941

In 1941, Amsterdam, the largest city in the Netherlands, housed more than 79,000 Jews. Approximately 10,000 of that population were foreign Jews hoping to escape the clutches of the Germans.

But the refugees did not find safety in the Netherlands. On February 22, 1941, the Nazis implemented their first arrest and deportation of Jews to the Buchenwald and Mauthausan concentration camps. By the end of the war, nearly 80 percent of Dutch Jews had perished.[3]

Otto sprang into action. First, he informed Hermann van Pels, his Pectacon business partner, of his plan. Hermann was Jewish and would join the Franks in hiding, along with his wife, Auguste, and their 15-year-old son, Peter. Otto then enlisted the help of Gies and her husband. They would be responsible for bringing last-minute clothes, books, and supplies to the Franks' hiding place because they would not arouse suspicion. Lastly, Otto told his family they needed to start packing.

That night, Anne and Margot shoved as many things as they could into an overnight bag. Margot stashed some of her favorite books. Anne gathered up her favorite Hollywood movie posters of actors and newspaper clippings of the Dutch royal family. The last thing she threw into her satchel was her beloved journal.

The next morning, a frightened Anne and the rest of her family woke up at 5:30 a.m. They piled on as many articles of clothing as they could bear—tights, shirts,

MIEP GIES, SAVIOR

Hermine Santrouschitz was born on February 15, 1909, in Vienna, Austria. After World War I broke out in 1914, Hermine and her family barely had enough to eat, and she became ill. When she turned 11, she was sent to Amsterdam to live with a foster family until she turned 18. The family nicknamed her Miep.

In 1933, 24-year-old Santrouschitz began working for Otto as an office assistant at Opekta. In 1941, she married Jan Gies and adopted his surname. When the Franks went into hiding, Gies and her husband were instrumental in smuggling food and supplies into the Secret Annex. But there was also something the Franks did not know: the Gieses also hid three other Jews in their own house, who survived.

Forty years after Anne's diary was published, Gies wrote a memoir entitled *Anne Frank Remembered: The Story of the Woman Who Helped to Hide the Frank Family*. Gies died on January 11, 2010. She was 100 years old.

Anne decorated the walls of her room in the Secret Annex with her collection of celebrity photos.

skirts, dresses, multiple pairs of underwear, and more. Then they made their apartment look as though they had fled in a hurry to Otto's relatives in Switzerland, leaving dishes in the sink and crumbs on the kitchen table. Margot ripped the yellow Jewish star off her jacket, and she and Gies biked across Amsterdam in the rain to a brick building along the Prinsengracht canal. Edith, Otto, and Anne followed on foot soon after.

Before long, all of the Franks had arrived at 263 Prinsengracht, where the offices of Gies & Co. had relocated a year earlier. Though none of them knew it at the time, they would never again return to 37 Merwedeplein as a fully intact family.

CHAPTER FIVE

THE SECRET ANNEX

When Anne first arrived at 263 Prinsengracht on the morning of July 6, 1942, she was momentarily confused. Was not this the building where her father worked? Were the Franks expected to live in the offices of Gies & Co.? Would she and Margot be forced to hide amidst boxes of spices and jars of pectin in the adjacent warehouse? Otto assured her that was not the case.

Followed by Edith and Margot, Otto led Anne up two flights of stairs to a hallway on the third floor. At the top of the stairs was a secret door camouflaged by a hinged bookcase. When Anne walked through it, she found herself in a separate area she never knew existed toward the rear of the building—a jumble of rooms she and her family would name the Secret Annex.

The Secret Annex consisted of six rooms. On the first floor of the annex was a dual-purpose room that would serve as the Frank family's living room during the day and Otto and Edith's bedroom at night. There

Soon after moving into the Annex, Anne wrote that her carefree school days were gone forever.

A worker at Gies & Co. built a bookcase to cover the entrance to the Secret Annex. The bookcase was attached to hinges and opened and closed like a door.

was also a study where Anne and Margot slept and a windowless bathroom for the household that included a sink and a closet containing a toilet. Upstairs, there was a kitchen that would be used as Hermann and Auguste's bedroom, a communal living and dining room, and a tiny bedroom for Peter. The top floor was an attic.

Each room was filled to the brim with boxes of clothes, linens, dishes, and books. The Franks' furniture from their old apartment was shoved haphazardly into every nook and cranny. For a year, Otto and Edith had collected supplies to bring to the Annex, fearing this day would eventually come. Now that it had arrived, Otto was anxious to unpack and get settled.

Over the next few days, there was a constant flurry of activity. Edith sewed curtains for every window in the Annex while Margot put 300 pounds (140 kg) of beans; cans of fruit, powdered milk, fish, and bratwurst; bottles of oil; bags of oatmeal; and jars of tomatoes into the cabinets.[1] Otto laid out the beds, tables, and chairs in each room and set up the radio they smuggled in with them. Anne distributed books to each member of the family and plastered movie posters on the wall next to her bed.

"The Annex is an ideal place to hide in," Anne wrote in her journal just before going to bed on July 11, after the last box was unpacked and stowed away. "It may be damp and lopsided, but there's probably not a more comfortable hiding place in all of Amsterdam. No, in all of Holland."[2]

BOOKS GALORE

Over the course of two years in captivity, Anne and her family had to keep themselves busy. They did so by reading piles of books smuggled in by Gies and Voskuijl. Some of the books they read included *Hedwig, The Cousin from Bremin, The Governess*, and *The Green* by Theodore Korner; *A Knock at the Door* by Ina Bakker Boudier; books by Charles Dickens; biographies of Emperor Charles V, Maria Theresa, and Galileo; and the Bible.

Turmoil in Hiding

Aside from having to remain completely quiet during daylight

Anne often wrote in her diary about fights with her mother, Edith.

hours, the first few months after the Franks and the Van Pelses moved in were relatively harmonious. Margot took correspondence courses in history, literature, French, Latin, and trigonometry to remain up to date in her studies. Peter spent much of his time in his room with his cat, Mouschi, flipping through comic books. The men huddled around the radio each afternoon at 1:00 p.m. to quietly listen to the news reports from the British Broadcasting Corporation (BBC), hoping to hear information about the Allied powers' progress in the fight against Hitler. Everyone looked forward to visits from Gies or Voskuijl, who snuck in groceries and supplies.

But even though she adored writing stories and reading books such as Nico van Suchtelen's *Eva's Youth* and Cissy van Marxveldt's Jooep ter Heul series, the only person who did not seem comfortable a majority of the time was Anne. The 13-year-old felt her mother was always picking on her, and the two bickered often. Anne had recurring nightmares of being shot by the Germans. And the more she tried to ignore her hypersensitive feelings, the more she felt antagonized by Hermann and Auguste.

> "The atmosphere is stifling, sluggish, leaden. Outside, you don't hear a single bird, and a deathly, oppressive silence hangs over the house and clings to me as if it were going to drag me into the deepest regions of the underworld. . . . I wander from room to room, climb up and down the stairs and feel like a songbird whose wings have been ripped off and who keeps hurling itself against the bars of its dark cage."[3]
>
> *—Anne Frank, October 29, 1943*

"They criticize everything, and I mean everything, about me: my behavior, my personality, my manners;

every inch of me, from head to toe and back again, is the subject of gossip and debate . . . According to the powers that be, I'm supposed to grin and bear it. But I can't! I have no intention of taking their insults lying down. I'll show them Anne Frank wasn't born yesterday!" she wrote in her diary on September 28, 1942. "Am I really as bad-mannered, headstrong, stubborn, pushy, stupid, lazy, as the [Van Pelses] say I am?"[4]

In November, the overall mood in the Secret Annex shifted. The novelty of their new home had worn off and was overshadowed by the constant fear of discovery. In addition, Pfeffer, a dentist and longtime acquaintance of the Franks, had joined the group in hiding. He moved into the room Anne shared with Margot, forcing Margot to relocate to Otto and Edith's bedroom on a makeshift cot. Meanwhile, Anne remained in her old room with Pfeffer. Space was now tighter than ever before. The Annex alternated between being too damp or too hot. Venturing outside was strictly forbidden. And the inhabitants' inability to open the curtains, flush the toilet, or even crack a window during business hours was making everyone especially cranky.

War Reaches Amsterdam

But no matter what was happening inside the walls of the Secret Annex, the events taking place outside were far worse. Long lines for bread and often rotten vegetables had become commonplace throughout Amsterdam; many families starved. Each household was given a monthly ration of heat and electricity, and those that went over their limits had to go without. Prices for simple things, such as shoelaces and thread, skyrocketed, while supplies of basic necessities vanished. The number of burglaries rose.

Piercing air-raid sirens sounded off at all hours. The roar of airplane engines and percussive machine-gun and antiaircraft fire became routine as British and German planes battled in the sky night after

BURGLED

Supplies ran short in Amsterdam during World War II. Many people began looting stores and vacant houses to make ends meet. In 1943 and 1944, the warehouse and storeroom of Gies & Co. were burgled twice by robbers who were never caught.

The robbery in April 1944 was especially scary for those in the Secret Annex. Anne and her family heard a loud crash, followed by shattering glass. Someone also came upstairs and rattled the bookcase. After that, the Franks, the Van Pelses, and Pfeffer were much quieter during daylight hours.

night. Buildings such as the fancy Carlton Hotel burned to rubble during the skirmishes. Neighbors snitched on old friends suspected of holding anti-Nazi beliefs. And throughout all of it, the gestapo took away Jews in droves. Rumors spread through the city that the captured Jews were being killed in gas chambers.

RATION CARDS

During World War II, supplies were scarce in Amsterdam and throughout Europe, the United Kingdom, and the United States. Imported luxuries, such as tea, bananas, and oranges, were virtually impossible to come by. Staples such as butter, salt, sugar, flour, and meat became hard to find, too.

To ensure everyone received an equal share, governments issued citywide mandates detailing how much of each item was allowed per person. Ration books were issued to keep track of each family's allotment.

Adults and children received tan-colored booklets that could be used to obtain things such as paper for school or two eggs and 12 ounces (340 g) of sugar for cooking. Pregnant women used green-colored books, which contained slightly more coupons that could be used for other items, such as milk or extra vegetables.

Long lines at shops were common. To keep spirits up, bread and alcohol were officially excluded from rationing, but supplies were often limited.

During their time in captivity, Anne and the rest of the residents in the Secret Annex were given food and household supplies by Miep and Jan Gies, who split their food ration coupons and made do with less or bought supplies off the black market. Though the Franks had hoarded resources prior to going into hiding, they were able to survive as long as they did because of this kindness.

"Night after night, green and gray military vehicles cruise the streets. They knock on every door, asking whether any Jews live there. If so, the whole family is immediately taken away," Anne wrote in her diary on November 19, 1942. "In the evenings when it's dark, I often see long lines of good, innocent people, accompanied by crying children, walking on and on, ordered about by a handful of men who bully and beat them until they nearly drop. No one is spared. The sick, the elderly, children, babies, and pregnant women—all are marched to their death."[5]

By the end of their first year in hiding, Anne and the other members of the Secret Annex were worn out from living in the shadow of fear. Emotions ran high. Fights among the residents of the Annex happened more frequently. But despite their harrowing reality, they went to bed each night determined to live another day—still in hiding, but nonetheless free.

"All we can do is wait, as calmly as possible, for it to end," Anne wrote in her journal. "Jews and Christians alike are waiting, the whole world is waiting."[6]

CHAPTER SIX

IN HIDING BUT STILL FREE

Beginning in the summer of 1943 and stretching into the spring of 1944, the members of the Secret Annex had a lot to celebrate. In July 1943, Italy's fascist dictator, Benito Mussolini, originally an ally of Hitler, was overthrown. Two months later, Italy willingly surrendered to Allied forces. Though Italy would not be declared its own free nation again until 1945, its cooperation with British and US troops meant the Germans were one step closer to defeat.

In November 1943, US president Franklin Delano Roosevelt, British prime minister Winston Churchill, and Soviet Union premier Joseph Stalin met in person for the first time in Tehran, Iran, to discuss their wartime strategies. They agreed to work together to beat back Germany in sustained and simultaneous attacks on both the eastern and western battlefronts.

After their first meeting, in 1943, Winston Churchill, *left*, Franklin Delano Roosevelt, *center*, and Joseph Stalin, *right*, met again in 1945 in Crimea, Soviet Union.

> "Listeners, an hour and fifteen minutes ago, just as I finished writing my daily report, we received the wonderful news of Italy's capitulation. I tell you, I never tossed my notes into the wastepaper basket with more delight than I did today!"[2]
> *—Dutch news broadcast from England, September 8, 1943*

Meanwhile, in Amsterdam and throughout the Netherlands, more and more Jews went into hiding, helped by Dutch sympathizers. Members of Dutch resistance groups forged identity cards, hoarded supplies, and scouted out secret shelters for those in need, all while recruiting other Christians to further the cause. "Going underground or into hiding has become as routine as the proverbial pipe and slippers that used to await the man of the house after a long day at work," Anne wrote in her journal on January 28, 1944. "It's amazing how much these generous and unselfish people do, risking their own lives to help and save others."[1]

The 14-year-old Anne and the rest of the Secret Annex's inhabitants understood the fight against Hitler and the Nazis was far from over. But news that the Allies were slowly but steadily gaining ground against Germany emboldened their spirits. If they could hold out for just a little while longer, maybe they could survive the war.

Inspiration Strikes

March 29, 1944, began just like any other day. The Franks, the Van Pelses, and Pfeffer had risen and had their breakfasts before the workers arrived below at Gies & Co. Margot studied geometry and shorthand, a method of handwriting that substitutes simple abbreviations or symbols for letters, words, or phrases. Anne worked on the genealogy charts she had created for the Austrian, Dutch, and Russian royal families.

DUTCH RESISTANCE GROUPS

During the Holocaust, between 25,000 and 30,000 Dutch Jews went into hiding. Two-thirds of this group managed to survive.[3] Their success was due in large part to the fearless Dutch citizens and Dutch resistance groups who risked their lives to help them.

Some Dutch resisters were members of the government the Germans put in place when the Nazis took control of the Netherlands. These embedded informants used their high government ranks to gather information about raids so they could warn Jews who were targeted for deportation.

Other members of the resistance recruited friends and relatives and formed organized underground groups, such as Free Netherlands. They snuck in food, extra ration books, clothing, and medicine to give to Jews in hiding. Some members helped smuggle Jews into countries free from German rule, such as Switzerland. The risks were high. If the Nazis caught the helpers, punishment was swift and severe: immediate death. But for members of the Dutch resistance, saving Jews' lives was worth the risk.

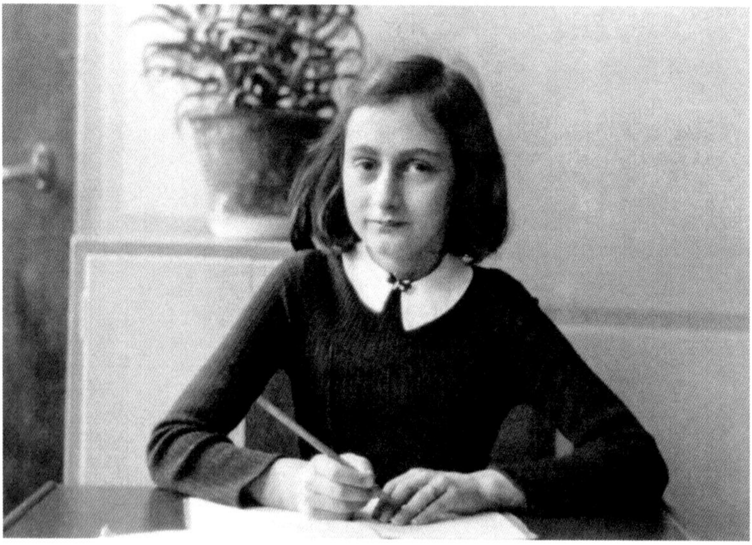

Anne hoped to someday write for a living.

Suddenly, an announcement on the radio caught Anne's ear.

Gerrit Bolkestein, the cabinet minister of education in the Dutch government, was discussing his intention to start collecting information on the suffering of the Dutch people under German occupation. He wanted letters and diary entries, photos and poems—anything that could serve as evidence of how Dutch citizens were coping. He was hoping to publish some of what he collected after the war.

Anne was ecstatic. She had the perfect record of events that had transpired over the previous two years—her journal. She immediately set to work on editing and modifying it. Over the next few months, she copied over what she had already written into a new notebook. She changed some of the people's names to protect their identities. She also took out anything she found too distasteful or babyish and added information to entries she felt were incomplete. Though she would keep on writing in her original diary, she wanted this new version to sound more mature and polished.

Revising her journal was hard work. But there was another reason why the process took Anne longer than she expected. Since New Year's Eve, she had started spending more time with the only other teenager in the house besides her sister—17-year-old Peter. Though she had found him annoying and aloof when he first moved in to the Secret Annex, Anne now found Peter to be charming. She cherished the open and honest talks they had started having in the attic each night, gazing out at her beloved chestnut tree, the moon, and

> "I need to have something besides a husband and children to devote myself to! I don't want to have lived in vain like most people. . . . I want to go on living even after my death! And that's why I'm so grateful to God for having given me this gift, which I can use to develop myself and to express all that's inside me. . . . Will I ever be able to write something great, will I ever become a journalist or a writer?"[4]
>
> *—Anne Frank, April 5, 1944*

the stars from the only window that allowed them a breath of fresh air.

"I think, Kitty, that true love may be developing in the Annex," Anne scribbled in her journal on March 22, 1944. "All those jokes about marrying Peter if we stayed here long enough weren't so silly after all. . . . I'm sure now that Peter loves me too; I just don't know in what way. I can't figure out if he wants only a good friend, or if he's attracted to me as a girl or as a sister."[5]

The Invasion Begins

On April 15, 1944, Anne celebrated her first kiss with Peter. Though she felt increasingly alienated from her family, especially her nagging mother, Anne felt more hopeful about the future than she had in months. Now she had a companion with whom she could share her deepest thoughts and feelings—about how she hated the Nazis and was terrified all the time of being found, about what sex would be like when it finally happened, about how much she longed to be a professional writer someday. It made being cooped up inside the Secret Annex slightly more bearable.

Then, just a few days shy of Anne's fifteenth birthday, a breakthrough occurred in the war.

As time went by in the Annex, Peter became more confident and outgoing, taking on odd jobs around the living space.

ANNE'S SEXUALITY

In the latter half of Anne's diary, many of the entries were devoted to her thoughts about her changing body. She longed to grow up and wondered when she might get her period.

Anne also wrote about her feelings regarding sex. Though she did not explicitly mention having intercourse, she did imagine what it might be like with Peter and often asked him questions regarding how certain sexual acts were performed. When the first versions of the diary were published, Otto edited out some of these entries, but they were later recovered and added back in.

On June 6, 1944—what would later be called D-Day—more than 155,000 British, Canadian, and US troops barreled onto the sandy shores of Normandy, France. Nearly 23,000 of them were US and British paratroopers who had landed behind German defensive lines the night before. Fifty thousand armored vehicles, 7,000 boats and warships, and 11,500 planes pummeled the German forces with bullets and bombs. There were many casualties during the initial attack over the next 24 hours, nearly 19,000 from both sides combined.[6] But after 19 days, the Allied forces triumphed, breaking the German lines. Weeks later, on August 25, they marched on to liberate Paris before crossing the border into Germany.

Anne and the others were overjoyed about the victory. Hitler and his troops were starting to lose their

With the Nazis being pushed back, Anne hoped life in Amsterdam would soon return to normal.

hold on the region. Approximately 107,000 Dutch Jews had been deported and killed in concentration camps in the two years since the Franks had gone into hiding.[7] But maybe the inhabitants of the Secret Annex would be saved now that Allied troops were on their way at last.

But help did not arrive in time. On the morning of August 4, 1944—three days after Anne's final diary entry—the German police were informed of the Secret Annex's location. The gestapo arrived at 263 Prinsengracht, barged up the stairs, tore away the bookcase, and arrested all inside. The Franks, the Van Pelses, and Pfeffer were taken into custody to await their fates.

CHAPTER SEVEN

THE DEADLIEST JOURNEY

On August 8, 1944, four days after their arrest, Anne and the other residents of the Secret Annex were forcefully placed on a transport bound for Westerbork, a detention center 80 miles (130 km) northeast of Amsterdam. Westerbork was where Dutch and German Jews were sent before being deported to extermination camps. When Anne and her family and friends arrived, they were shocked by what they saw: dozens of identical buildings in rows, watchtowers with guards carrying machine guns, a barbed-wire fence that lined the perimeter of the complex, and thousands of malnourished prisoners milling about.

Almost immediately after they stepped off the train, the new arrivals were separated into clusters. The Franks, the Van Pelses, and Pfeffer were all assigned to the punishment block because they had not voluntarily reported to German authorities when they received

Despite being captured, Anne and the other members of the Secret Annex remained optimistic on the train ride to Westerbork.

WESTERBORK

Westerbork served as the main transport center for Jews during the Holocaust. From July 1942 until September 1944, the Germans deported 97,776 Jews from Westerbork: 54,930 to Auschwitz in 68 transports, 34,313 to Sobibor in 19 transports, 4,771 to the Theresienstadt ghetto in 7 transports, and 3,762 to the Bergen-Belsen concentration camp in 9 transports.[1] Most of those deported to Auschwitz and Sobibor were gassed immediately upon arrival.

The last transport from Westerbork to Auschwitz was on September 3, 1944—the day the Secret Annex inhabitants were deported. Westerbork was liberated on April 12, 1945, by Canadian troops. All but 876 prisoners had either died or been transferred to other camps.[2]

their call-up notices. They had been found while in hiding. Unlike prisoners in the regular barracks, they and other "convict" Jews were not given soap or allowed to keep their own clothes or shoes. Instead, they were issued ratty, striped overalls and stiff wooden shoes that did not fit. They were forced to work long hours doing hard labor.

The group struggled to get by at Westerbork. There was very little food to eat and every day was exhausting. Edith, Margot, and Anne squeezed onto one twin-sized bunk each night to sleep, and every morning at 5:00 a.m. the job of taking apart old batteries began. "We had to chop open the batteries with a hammer and a chisel and then throw the tar in one basket and the carbon bars, which we had to remove, into another basket. We had to take off the metal caps with a screwdriver, and they went into a third basket," remembered Jannie Brandes-Brilleslijper, a fellow prisoner. "In addition to getting terribly dirty from the work, we all began to cough because it gave off a certain kind of dust."[3]

Anne and the rest of the members of the Annex remained at Westerbork for almost a month. Then, on September 3, 1944, they were crammed into a freight train along with 1,011 other prisoners—498 women, 442 men, and 79 children total.[4] None of the prisoners knew where they were going. But at least the members of the Secret Annex were still together.

Arrival at Auschwitz

For three days and three nights, the train clattered through the Dutch countryside and into Poland near the German border. Straw covered the floor and the 70 people packed inside each car were forced to stand at all times. The stench—from sweating bodies, from the single pail used for human waste, from the vomit—was overwhelming. Some people tried to keep track of time by watching the sun rise and set through the tiny holes

AN UNWILLING HELPER

In most concentration camps, kapos, or privileged prisoners, were chosen by Nazi guards to help keep order. Some were forced to spy and report on their own family members. Others were tasked with running the crematoriums and were forced to kill their own friends.

Trude Levi, a prisoner at Buchenwald, was asked to be a kapo. She refused. "I wanted to survive but not at any price. I had a choice about how to behave. Most girls would have been overjoyed to obtain such a privileged position, as it meant extra rations and other perquisites. I did not want to live without my integrity."[6]

in the train's ceiling. Some people died along the way. "As we rode, Anne would not move from the window," Otto later recalled. "It was summer outside. Meadows, stubble fields and villages flew by. The telephone wires along the right of way curved up and down along the windows. After two years [in hiding], it was like freedom for her."[5]

Then, before dawn on September 6, the transport suddenly lurched to a stop. Each car's door was flung open and chaos erupted from both inside and out. Dogs barked viciously, saliva dripping from their teeth. Bright spotlights glared. Currents from the electrified barbed-wire fence surrounding the camp sizzled. Kapos, or favored prisoners who helped the Germans maintain discipline, milled back and forth to ensure all was in order. "*Aussteigen! Schnell! Schnell!*"

At Auschwitz, Nazi guards immediately selected which Jews would be put to work and which would be sent to the gas chambers.

("Get off! Hurry! Hurry!") yelled inmates in striped uniforms as the newcomers jumped off the train.[7] Anne and the rest of the Secret Annex inhabitants had arrived at Auschwitz, one of the Nazis' deadliest concentration camp complexes.

Immediately after the prisoners disembarked from the train, they were separated into groups, men on one side and women on the other. Those who were ill, too young, too old, pregnant, or generally unfit to work were then separated into a third group on the left. This group—549 out of the original 1,019—was ordered to undress.[8] They were handed towels and tiny bars of soap, and sent off to a building marked "showers." There, the frightened and naïve prisoners huddled together as a German guard fed toxic hydrogen cyanide into a vent in the ceiling. Moments later, the gas did its job, killing everyone inside. The bodies were burned in the adjacent crematorium.

The group that had been sent to the right, including the eight inhabitants of the Secret Annex, survived the first night. Otto, Hermann, Peter, and Pfeffer were taken to the main labor camp. Auguste, Edith, Margot,

IDENTIFICATION TATTOOS

With thousands of people cycling through the many concentration camps scattered throughout Europe and the East on any given day, it was often difficult to keep track of each prisoner's identity. In most cases, anyone who arrived at a camp remained anonymous. But at Auschwitz, the practice was different.

Auschwitz inmates who were assigned to work duty were issued serial numbers, which were placed on their uniforms. Those who were too ill or too weak were sent directly to the gas chamber without being given a number.

This practice soon changed when the Nazis realized they needed a way to identify prisoners if their clothing was removed, mainly after their deaths. Guards started branding each inmate's body with his or her identification number as soon as he or she arrived at the camp and was selected for work duty.

The first tattoos were made using a metal stamp applied to the chest. Later, they were drawn using a needle and ink on the left forearm. By the time Auschwitz was liberated in 1945, more than 400,000 identification numbers had been given out and tattooed.[9]

and Anne were sent to Birkenau, a section of Auschwitz located on the other side of the railroad tracks. Before the women departed, each of them had an identification number tattooed on her left forearm. It would be the last time the men and women from the Annex saw one another.

At Death's Door

Anne, Margot, and Edith spent the next two months struggling to survive the dehumanizing conditions at Birkenau. Their heads were shaved and their bodies disinfected for lice. Each morning they rose for roll call before sunrise and stood in line until everyone's name was called, sometimes for four hours at a time in the rain and sleet. Then they toiled away at endless chores—digging grass into useless piles, doling out what little scraps of food they were given, cleaning the buckets used for toilets. At night, they and hundreds of other inmates were crammed into barracks built for 40 people.

"Anne often stood next to me [at roll call] and Margot was close by," said fellow prisoner Ronnie Goldstein-van Cleef. "[Anne] was very calm and quiet and somewhat withdrawn. The fact that they had

Women were crammed into crude barracks at Birkenau and other concentration camps.

ended up there had affected her profoundly—that was obvious."[10]

The food at Birkenau was virtually inedible—stale bread made with sawdust, watery turnip soup, and occasionally a slice of sausage. Drinking water was often polluted with bacteria. Toilets consisted of a slab of wood with holes over a series of buckets that were rarely emptied. Consequently, many people grew sick with dysentery, a deadly type of fever. Anne came down with scabies, an itchy, irritating skin disease.

Each week, everyone in the camp was subjected to a selection process. Those who were too thin or unwell were gassed to make room for incoming prisoners. Those who appeared strong were either forced to continue working or shipped to other camps or sometimes factories to make munitions for Nazi troops.

At the end of October 1944, it was Anne and Margot's turn to be picked. "There they stood for that moment, naked and bald. Anne looked straight at us with her innocent eyes, and then they were gone," recalled Rosa de Winter-Levy, a Holocaust survivor who witnessed the roll call that day. "We weren't able to see what happened to them next. We heard Mrs. Frank cry out: 'The children! Oh God. . . .'"[11] The next day, the Frank sisters were transferred to Bergen-Belsen concentration camp in northern Germany. Their mother, who was too frail to make the journey, remained at Auschwitz. Lost without her

ANNE'S POWER

Holocaust prisoners suffered unimaginable horrors during their internment at concentration camps. But many of Anne's fellow inmates who survived the Holocaust attest to her unfailing optimism and dedication to helping others.

In the 1958 book *Anne Frank: A Portrait of Courage,* Rootje de Winter—a prisoner who became close with the Frank women at Westerbork, Auschwitz, and Bergen-Belsen—shared her memories of Anne: "To the last also [Anne] was moved by the dreadful things the rest of us had somehow become hardened to. Who bothered to look when the flames shot up into the sky at night from the crematoriums? Who was troubled that every day new people were being selected and gassed? Most of us were beyond feeling. But not Anne."[12]

daughters, she died there on January 6, 1945, just ten days before her forty-fifth birthday.

Anne and Margot held on at Bergen-Belsen for five months, despite intense overcrowding. Anne even reunited with Hanneli Goslar, her old friend from childhood. During their time together, Goslar saved some of her own scraps of food to share with Anne and her sister, who had fallen ill. But the lack of food and water, intense cold, and rampant germs ultimately did the Frank sisters in.

"At a certain moment in her final days, Anne stood in front of me, wrapped in a blanket. . . . She told me that she had such a horror of the lice and fleas in her clothes and that she had thrown all of her clothes away," recalled Brandes-Brilleslijper, who had followed the Frank girls

BERGEN-BELSEN

Bergen-Belsen was not an extermination camp. Constructed in 1940 and in operation until 1945, it housed prisoners of war, political prisoners, criminals, Roma, Jehovah's Witnesses, homosexuals, and Jews, many of whom had been evacuated from other concentration camps.

Thousands of people died at Bergen-Belsen because of overcrowding and the rampant spread of disease. In mid-1944, the camp housed 7,300 prisoners. At the end of that year, the number had doubled. By the time the British liberated the camp on April 15, 1945, the population had soared to 60,000. During its existence, nearly 50,000 inmates died at Bergen-Belsen.[13] Two of them were Anne and Margot.

In the weeks following Bergen-Belsen's liberation, thousands of victims continued to die from typhus.

to Auschwitz, then Bergen-Belsen. "It was the middle of winter and she was wrapped in one blanket. I gathered up everything I could find to give her so that she was dressed again."[14] Three days after that incident, on March 9, 1945, 19-year-old Margot died from typhus. Anne, who was 15 years old, passed away a few days later. Their bodies were dumped in a communal grave. British soldiers liberated Bergen-Belsen one month later, on April 15.

CHAPTER EIGHT

LIBERATED AT LAST

By the end of 1944, Hitler was no longer in control of the war. The Germans were on the run as Allied forces closed in on them from all sides. In August and September, the Allies liberated Paris and Pisa, Italy. In October, the Germans retreated from Greece and British troops liberated Athens, the nation's capital. In a brutally cold December, Germany waged the costly Battle of the Bulge, trying but failing to breach Allied lines and regain control of Belgium and Luxembourg. The Nazis lost more than 100,000 men.[1]

The more ground Germany lost, the more worried Hitler became about what the Allies might find once they encountered the 20,000 concentration camps scattered across the region.[2] As early as the summer of 1944, he issued orders for the decommissioning and deconstruction of any camp that might lie in the Allies' path. Electrified fences were torn down. Gas chambers and crematoriums were demolished. Paper records were destroyed and prisoners' valuables were shipped back to

Despite heavy early losses, Allied troops rallied to deal the Nazis a critical defeat during the Battle of the Bulge.

Germany to be used by German citizens. Hundreds of thousands of dead bodies were taken from mass graves and burned in open pits.

Prisoners who were still alive at these camps were dealt with systematically. Those who were too old or sick were gassed or left to die of starvation. Anyone well enough to work was forced to walk, sometimes thousands of miles, through rain, snow, and sleet to still-operational camps, such as Mauthausen, further inside German territory. Many died on the way.

On January 16, 1945, Soviet planes attacked Auschwitz. As the Soviet ground forces inched closer, Nazi guards ordered the evacuation of the remaining 60,000 prisoners. At least

TREASURED REMNANTS

When Jews, Roma, and other non-Germans were deported to concentration camps, many of their valuables were taken from them before they were killed and were repurposed for the war effort. Gold teeth and wedding rings were melted down and deposited as currency into Nazi bank accounts. Hair was often sold to make mattresses, chair cushions, or blankets.

When Auschwitz was liberated in January 1945, a stockpile of prisoners' belongings were discovered, including a building packed full of men's suits, more than 800,000 women's dresses, 43,000 pairs of shoes, and 14,000 pounds (6,350 kg) of hair. Some of these materials were either incinerated or broken down to be recycled for other purposes. Others remain at Auschwitz and other Holocaust memorials around the world as part of museum exhibits.[3]

15,000 of them died on the way to other concentration camps.[4] Those who were too frail stayed behind. When Auschwitz was finally liberated on January 27, 1945, less than 1 percent of the more than 1.1 million Jews and the 200,000 non-Jewish prisoners of war who had passed through the camp's gates were alive.[5] Otto Frank was one of them.

PETER'S DEATH MARCH

In January 1945, just prior to the liberation of Auschwitz, nearly 60,000 prisoners were forced to evacuate, including Peter.[6]

Though he was relatively strong when he left Auschwitz, his health deteriorated during the bitterly cold and wet 373-mile (600 km) journey. When he arrived at Mauthausen concentration camp in Austria on January 25, he was exhausted. The camp was liberated on May 5, but Peter died before the rescuers arrived. The exact date of his death is unknown.

Returning Home

For four months, Otto stayed under the care of his Soviet liberators, slowly regaining his health and strength. In May, he began the long and arduous journey back to Amsterdam. He traveled by train, boat, and car. When he finally arrived home, it was June 3, 1945.

Otto went immediately to see his old friends and business associates, Miep and Jan Gies. He had learned of his wife's death at Auschwitz and was crushed by the news. But Miep and Jan provided a much-needed link to his old life. "My first path was to Miep and her husband and, because I no longer had a home, I stayed there," Otto said in an interview years later. "It was then that I discovered that she and Bep had never been arrested and that my friends Kleiman and Kugler had come back from the concentration camps to which they had been sent. We all had lots of stories of our sad experiences. They mourned the death of my wife with me, but we were hopeful that the children would return."[7]

A SERENDIPITOUS REUNION

Otto Frank was heartbroken after learning his family had not survived the concentration camps. On his return trip home to Amsterdam, however, he met an old friend, Elfriede "Fritzi" Geiringer, who had also survived, along with her daughter, Eva.

In the years after the Holocaust, Otto and Geiringer were a great comfort to each other. While mourning the deaths of their families, they fell in love. In 1953, Otto and Geiringer married and moved to Basel, Switzerland. For the rest of their lives, they worked to publish Anne's diaries and promote racial tolerance throughout the world.

Word had not yet reached Amsterdam that Anne and Margot had perished at Bergen-Belsen three months earlier. Otto resumed work at his old company, and in every spare moment, he and the Gieses tried to find information about the girls' whereabouts. They placed

After the war, Otto, *center*, reunited with Gies, *front left*; Voskuijl, *front right*; Kugler, *back right*, and Kleiman, *back left*.

ads in newspapers and checked the Red Cross's lists of people missing and dead. They contacted survivors. They hoped and prayed for the impossible.

But on July 18, Otto learned of the girls' deaths from Jannie Brandes-Brilleslijper, now a nurse in Rotterdam, the Netherlands. He was devastated and inconsolable. For weeks, stunned, he walked around Amsterdam, knowing everyone in his immediate family was gone. He thought his life would never have meaning again.

An Important Gift

After news of the girls' deaths reached Gies, she knew there was only one thing she could do to raise Otto's spirits. She went into her office, reached into her desk drawer, and pulled out the bundle of Anne's journals and notebooks.

JANNIE BRANDES-BRILLESLIJPER

Jannie Brandes-Brilleslijper was the last known person to have seen Anne and Margot alive before they died in the spring of 1945. She worked as a nurse in Bergen-Belsen. She provided clothing, food, and medicine to fellow inmates.

"Maybe it was a 'sister complex' that attracted our attention to the Frank girls. . . . [My sister and I] had sort of motherly feelings for them," Brandes-Brilleslijper later wrote in a memoir she published with five other survivors. "Anne and Margot, they had each other. But they didn't have enough resistance to fight. We were a little older and we knew what we were fighting for."[8]

The 27-year-old Brandes-Brilleslijper and her older sister, Lientje, became friends with the Frank sisters on August 8, 1944, on their way to Westerbork. But before going to the camp, Brandes-Brilleslijper lived a much different life than Anne. She was married to Bob Brandes, a non-Jew, and had two children. She was also part of the Jewish resistance. She created false identification papers for Jews hoping to escape the Nazis. And she produced an illegal newspaper out of her home.

After Bergen-Belsen was liberated in 1945, Brandes-Brilleslijper returned with her sister to Amsterdam, where they were reunited with their families. She died on August 15, 2003. She was 86 years old at the time of her death.

Otto returned to find Anne's room and the rest of the Secret Annex cleared out.

"I took out all the papers, placing the little red-orange checkered diary on top, and carried everything into Mr. Frank's office," she wrote in her autobiography, years later. "Frank was sitting at his desk, his eyes murky with shock. I held out the diary and the papers to him. I said, 'Here is your daughter Anne's legacy to you.'"[9]

The sight of Gies's gift overwhelmed Otto. He sat in his office with tears in his eyes and the door closed for a long, long time. Weeks later, when he could finally muster up the courage, he began reading. Over the next few months, Otto read and reread his daughter's words. He was touched by her spunk and her honesty.

There was so much he never knew about Anne. Some of it—her ongoing animosity toward her mother, her dislike of Hermann and Auguste—was disheartening to learn. But the other parts—her crush on Peter, her love of life and passion for writing—were priceless. "I began to read slowly, only a few pages each day, more would have been impossible, as I was overwhelmed by painful memories," Otto later said. "For me, it was a revelation. There was revealed a completely different Anne to the child that I had lost. I had no idea of the depths of her thoughts and feelings."[10]

It was then Otto realized he should not be the only one with access to his daughter's thoughts. The passion she felt for writing and describing her feelings was clearly evident. Otto knew Anne's words and wisdom needed to be shared. The world had to be told about the horrors he, his family, and millions of other Jews had suffered under Hitler and the Nazis. Anne's strength and belief in the inherent goodness of most people needed to live on.

Otto made it his mission to publish Anne's story for the world to read.

CHAPTER NINE

ANNE'S LEGACY

On May 7, 1945, Germany signed an unconditional surrender agreement, officially ending World War II in Europe. Millions of people around the world rejoiced that Hitler's brutal, murderous reign had come to an end. In August 1945, the United States forced Japan to surrender by dropping atomic bombs on the cities of Hiroshima and Nagasaki. Japan's emperor conceded in a radio address on August 15. The official agreement was signed on September 2. The war was finally over.

The victory was bittersweet for Otto, Miep and Jan, and the rest of those who had helped the inhabitants of the Secret Annex. Their side had won, but they, like many, had lost so much. Holocaust survivors had to live with the knowledge that most of their loved ones would not be coming home again. Rebuilding their lives from scratch was often too difficult a task to bear.

But with the aid of friends and some relatives who had waited out the war in Switzerland, Otto worked

A symbolic grave in Bergen-Belsen memorializes Anne and Margot.

hard to recover. He rekindled a friendship, which later blossomed into a life-long romance, with former neighbor and Auschwitz survivor Elfriede Geiringer, whose husband and son had also died in the camps. And he spent his days translating, editing, and splicing together Anne's diaries and sharing entries with editors and journalists. He was convinced that it was his purpose to carry out Anne's undying wish to have her journals published.

EVA SCHLOSS

Eva Schloss was 23 years old when her mother married Otto Frank on November 10, 1953. The marriage made her Anne Frank's posthumous stepsister.

Though Eva and Anne had been in the same class at school growing up, they had had little in common and had not been close. Later, when Eva survived the war, she was devastated to learn of her brother and father's deaths and resented her mother's union with Otto:

> *After my mother married Otto I started to be introduced as Anne Frank's step-sister. I thought: I am still a person, I have a name and I lived through the same things she did. It was a difficult time . . . to see my mother so happy too when I had adored my father.*

Eva Schloss wrote her own memoirs about her experiences at the concentration camps during the Holocaust. Ultimately, she learned to embrace her connection to her stepsister and to move beyond her past. "[Now] I am really a very happy person and I know I was very lucky to survive, to get out and to have a family."[1]

Published to the World

On April 3, 1946, an article about Anne's writings by Dutch historian Jan Romein, who had received the edited and compiled manuscript from a journalist colleague, ran on the front page of *Het Parool*, a Dutch newspaper. "To me, however, this apparently inconsequential diary by a child . . . stammered out in a child's voice, embodies all the hideousness of fascism, more so than all the evidence at Nuremberg put together," Romein wrote.[2]

The article attracted the attention of many Dutch publishers. After months of meetings and revisions, to the delight of Otto and Gies, a version of Anne's diary was

DIFFERENT VERSIONS

More than one version of Anne's diary was published. There are now three versions available to English readers. Version A includes the red-and-tan-checkered cloth journal and the three additional notebooks Anne kept during her two years in hiding. Some of the original entries from the notebooks were lost during the war, including many that were written during 1943. Version B contains material Anne created after hearing the radio announcement from Education Minister Bolkestein. These excerpts were edited and revised drafts of Anne's original diary entries. Version C contains both material from versions A and B. This is the version Otto created once he returned home from Auschwitz. Published in 1989, *The Diary of Anne Frank: The Critical Edition* contains versions A, B, and C.

published in the Netherlands on June 25, 1947. Three thousand copies were made. The book was called *Het Achterhuis* (*The Secret Annex*).

Reviews of *Het Achterhuis* were mostly positive. "Since the Liberation, I have read hardly anything that is as pure and moving as Anne Frank's diary," one stated.[3] As word of its existence spread, the book was in such high demand the publisher had to print additional copies in December. Ten thousand more were printed in February 1948.

By 1952, Anne's diary could be bought in Germany, France, and the United Kingdom. The US edition, retitled *Anne Frank: The Diary of a Young Girl*, was published that same year, after it had been rejected by ten publishers. It contained a preface written by Eleanor Roosevelt, widow of US president Franklin Delano Roosevelt, and soon became a best seller.

ALIVE AGAIN

Even though Gies had guarded Anne's diary during the war, she had never read it. It brought back too many bad memories. When the book was published in 1947, Gies finally agreed to read it.

"I read the whole diary without stopping," Gies said later. "From the first word, I heard Anne's voice come back to speak to me from where she had gone. I lost track of time. Anne's voice tumbled out of the book, so full of life, moods, curiosity, feelings. She was no longer gone and destroyed. She was alive again in my mind."[4]

Anne's original diaries are on display in Amsterdam, though facsimiles appear in museums around the world.

Beyond the Page

Since the book's initial publication in 1947, *Het Achterhuis* has been published in 70 languages worldwide.[5] More than 30 million copies have been sold in 60 countries and counting.[6] The book has touched the hearts of countless students and teachers and has become mandatory reading in many classrooms across the globe.

Anne's words have spread beyond the printed page, too. In 1955, the play *The Diary of Anne Frank* opened on Broadway and won a New York Critic's Circle Award for Best Play, a Tony Award, and the Pulitzer Prize for Drama. The first movie adaptation, filmed in 1959, won three Academy Awards, including Shelly Winters's

ANNE FRANK IN THE WORLD

In 1994, an exhibit from the Anne Frank House journeyed to South Africa to promote tolerance and peace following the country's emergence from government-enforced segregation, which lasted from 1948 to 1994. More than 100,000 South Africans visited the exhibition as it traveled through six different cities.[7]

Former president of South Africa Nelson Mandela gave a speech during the exhibit's opening ceremony in Johannesburg on August 15. In it, he spoke of the impact Anne's words had on him during the 27 years he spent in prison for allegedly conspiring to overthrow the government. "Some of us read Anne Frank's diary," Mandela said. "We derived much encouragement from it. It kept our spirits high and reinforced our confidence in the invincibility of the cause of freedom and justice."[8]

Best Supporting Actress win for her portrayal of Auguste van Pels. Anne's story has also inspired a slew of other productions, including two television series—one in 1987 and another in 2009—and a few short documentaries.

Now, those inspired by Anne's words who are interested in learning more about her life and legacy can actually visit the Secret Annex, all of 263 Prinsengracht, and the building next door, which were transformed into a museum in 1960, called the Anne Frank House. Visitors can retrace Anne's first steps into the Secret Annex in 1942 and imagine what it must have felt like for her to be trapped inside, writing in her diary and fearing for her life.

"The spiritual value of the house is very great. Thousands of people from all over the world have visited it the last years, many bringing flowers. And to be in the rooms where everything Anne wrote about had happened made an unforgettable impression on them," Otto said in a speech on March 24, 1959, months before the museum officially opened. "But more must be achieved. It is not enough that people are moved and come to think about all the terrible events. We must do more."[9]

On May 3, 1961, Otto turned part of the museum into an educational center for children and teens called the International Youth Centre at Anne Frank House. Here, young people can learn about the Holocaust through exhibits, lectures, and interactive performances. They can also participate in discussions about how to prevent such things from happening in the future

A TREE PLANTED

In 2009, the Anne Frank Center USA launched a nationwide program called the Sapling Project, in honor of the chestnut tree Anne treasured so dearly that was located outside her window at the Secret Annex. Before the tree became riddled with disease and fell down in a windstorm in 2010, it had lived to be more than 170 years old.

Before the tree's demise, saplings were taken and planted at 11 different locations across the United States, including one on the western front lawn of the US Capitol. That tree was planted on April 30, 2009.

by promoting racial and religious tolerance and peace throughout the world.

Anne Frank Lives On

Otto Frank, the last living member of the Secret Annex, died in Basel, Switzerland, on August 19, 1980. He was 91 years old. For the last 35 years of his life, he worked diligently to ensure the memory of his daughter would live on for years to come. He answered thousands of letters from people around the world who were touched by Anne's diary. And in 1963, he founded the Anne Frank Fonds, a foundation dedicated to financing charitable projects in Anne's honor.

Anne did not survive the Holocaust. She died a slow, ghastly death not because of anything she had done wrong but because of her religion. Similar to many Jews, she was singled out and persecuted by a group of hateful oppressors. For the Nazis, prejudice and fear took precedence over logic and willingness to embrace people as equals regardless of religion, skin color, or racial background.

Anne wrote in her diary, "I shall not remain insignificant, I shall work in the world for mankind."[10] Despite her cruel fate, Anne has more than fulfilled

A large mural commemorates Anne in Berlin, Germany.

this promise. Her diary serves as a powerful reminder both of the terrible things people are capable of and of humanity's lasting resilience. Her words live on as a symbol of courage and hope for all humankind.

TIMELINE

1929
Annelies Marie Frank is born on June 12 in Frankfurt am Main, Germany.

1929
The US stock market crash sets off a financial crisis around the world; German banks, including Otto Frank's, are some of the hardest hit.

1933
Adolf Hitler is appointed chancellor of Germany on January 30.

1933
The Franks immigrate to Amsterdam, the Netherlands, to escape anti-Semitism in Germany.

1933
Otto forms the Dutch Opekta Company, a pectin business.

1938

Nazis attack Jewish-owned businesses, synagogues, and homes in a night of violence called Kristallnacht, "Night of Broken Glass."

1939

Germany invades Poland on September 1; World War II begins.

1940

The Netherlands surrenders on May 14 after four days of German attacks.

1942

Anne writes in her diary for the first time on June 12, her 13th birthday; the Franks go into hiding on July 6.

1944

Anne hears a radio broadcast calling for written accounts of Dutch suffering under German occupation. She starts revising her diary.

1944

On June 6, known as D-Day, the Allies begin to invade Nazi-occupied territory.

TIMELINE

1944

On August 4, the Nazis arrest the Franks and the other four residents of the Secret Annex; they are sent to Westerbork on August 8.

1944

The residents of the Secret Annex board the train to Auschwitz on September 3.

1944

Anne and Margot are transferred to Bergen-Belsen concentration camp in October.

1945

Edith dies of starvation at Auschwitz in January; Anne and Margot die within a few days of each other in March at Bergen-Belsen after coming down with typhus; Peter van Pels dies at Mauthausen.

1945

Otto, the only surviving member of the Frank family, is liberated from Auschwitz on January 27; he returns to Amsterdam on June 3.

1945
Germany surrenders; World War II officially ends on September 2.

1947
Anne's diary is published in Dutch with the title *Het Achterhuis* (*The Secret Annex*).

1952
Anne Frank: The Diary of a Young Girl is published in English in the United States.

1960
The Anne Frank House, a museum and memorial to the Secret Annex, opens in Amsterdam.

1980
Otto dies on August 19.

ESSENTIAL FACTS

Date of Birth

June 12, 1929

Place of Birth

Frankfurt am Main, Germany

Date of Death

March 1945 (exact date unknown)

Parents

Otto and Edith Frank

Education

The Sixth Montessori School
The Jewish Lyceum

Societal Contribution

After Anne's death in 1945, her diary lives on as a shining example of human strength and dignity. Both the Anne Frank Fonds and the International Youth Centre at Anne Frank House, founded in her honor by her father, work toward promoting peace and tolerance throughout the world.

Conflicts

Because they were Jewish, Anne and her family were considered racially inferior and therefore subhuman by Adolf Hitler and his Nazi Party. Leading up to the Holocaust, millions of European Jews, including the Franks, were forced to put up with debilitating restrictions and to endure countless acts of violent aggression. Six million Jews were ruthlessly killed in what Hitler called the Final Solution between 1939 and 1945.

Publications and Adaptations

The first Dutch edition of Anne's diary was posthumously published in 1947. After two subsequent printings, demand for the book increased. It was published in Germany in 1950, followed by the English version in 1952. A slew of adaptions soon followed, including a Pulitzer Prize–winning play on Broadway in 1955 and an Academy Award–winning movie in 1959. In addition to becoming mandatory reading in classrooms around the world, Anne's diary has sold more than 30 million copies in 60 countries.

Quote

"Writing in a diary is a really strange experience for someone like me. Not only because I've never written anything before, but because it seems to me that later on neither I nor anyone else will be interested in the musings of a 13-year-old school girl. Oh well, it doesn't matter. . . . Paper has more patience than people." —*Anne Frank*

GLOSSARY

anti-Semitism
Hostility toward or prejudice against Jews.

boycott
To refuse to have dealings with, usually in order to express disapproval or to force acceptance of certain conditions.

communist
A person who believes in communism, an economic system based on the elimination of private ownership of factories, land, and other means of economic production.

concentration camp
A type of prison where large numbers of people who are not soldiers are kept during a war and are usually forced to live in bad conditions.

crematorium
A furnace for burning bodies or a building containing such a furnace.

emigrate
To leave one's place of residence or country to live elsewhere.

fascist
A person who believes in a government structure in which one person has total power and opposition is suppressed.

Holocaust
The slaughter of European civilians, especially Jews, by the Nazis during World War II.

Jehovah's Witness

A member of a religious group that believes in the imminent destruction of the world's wickedness and that seeks to evangelize to others.

Jewish

Someone who is descended from Jewish people or who participates in the culture surrounding Judaism, the religion developed among the ancient Hebrews that stresses faithfulness to the laws of the Torah.

munition

Material used in war, especially weapons and ammunition.

pectin

A substance in some fruits that makes fruit jellies thick when the fruit is cooked.

posthumous

Happening after someone's death.

synagogue

The house of worship and communal center of a Jewish congregation.

typhus

A serious disease carried by small insects and which causes high fever, headache, and a dark red rash.

ADDITIONAL RESOURCES

Selected Bibliography

Frank, Anne. *The Diary of Anne Frank: The Revised Critical Edition.* New York: Doubleday, 2003. Print.

Gies, Miep, and Alison Leslie Gold. *Anne Frank Remembered: The Story of the Woman Who Helped to Hide the Frank Family.* New York: Simon, 1987. Print.

Müller, Melissa. *Anne Frank: The Biography.* New York: Metropolitan, 1998. Print.

Further Readings

Gitlin, Martin. *The Holocaust.* Minneapolis, MN: Abdo, 2011. Print.

Vander Hook, Sue. *Adolf Hitler.* Minneapolis, MN: Abdo, 2011. Print.

Websites

To learn more about Essential Lives, visit **booklinks.abdopublishing.com**. These links are routinely monitored and updated to provide the most current information available.

Places to Visit

The Anne Frank Center USA
44 Park Place
New York, NY 10007
212-431-7993
http://annefrank.com/
Created by Otto Frank in 1959 as a US-based partner to the Anne Frank House, the center features exhibits that explore the dangers of intolerance and racial discrimination.

Anne Frank House
Prinsengracht 263-267
1016 GV Amsterdam
Netherlands
+31 20 556 7100
http://www.annefrank.org/en/Museum/
The building where Anne and seven others lived in hiding from 1942 to 1944 now displays artifacts from the Secret Annex as well as new exhibits every six months.

The United States Holocaust Memorial Museum
100 Raoul Wallenberg Place SW
Washington, DC 20024
202-488-0400
http://www.ushmm.org/
The museum is the United States' official memorial to the Holocaust. Historical artifacts, video footage, and informative educational programs tell the story of the Franks and the 6 million Jews who were killed during the Holocaust.

SOURCE NOTES

Chapter 1. Betrayed

1. Miep Gies and Alison Leslie Gold. *Anne Frank Remembered: The Story of the Woman Who Helped to Hide the Frank Family.* New York: Simon, 1987. Print. 195.

2. Ibid. 196.

3. Ibid. 197.

4. Thomas A. Hughes. "World War II." *Encyclopaedia Britannica.* Encyclopaedia Britannica, 23 May 2014. Web. 1 Dec. 2015.

Chapter 2. A Tumultuous Childhood

1. Anne Frank. *The Diary of a Young Girl: The Definitive Edition.* New York: Doubleday, 1995. Print. 51.

2. "Mein Kampf." *Encyclopaedia Britannica.* Encyclopaedia Britannica, 20 Feb. 2014. Web. 1 Dec. 2015.

3. "Friendship with the Frank Family." *MiepGies.nl.* Miep Gies: Her Own Story, 2014. Web. 1 Dec. 2015.

4. "A New Start." *AnneFrank.org.* Anne Frank House, 2014. Web. 1 Dec. 2015.

Chapter 3. The Seeds of the Holocaust

1. "The Evian Conference." *USHMM.org.* United States Holocaust Memorial Museum, 2014. Web. 1 Dec. 2015.

2. "Kristallnacht: The November 1938 Pogroms." *USHMM.org.* United States Holocaust Memorial Museum, 2014. Web. 1 Dec. 2015.

3. "Kristallnacht: A Nationwide Pogrom: November 9–10, 1938." *USHMM.org.* United States Holocaust Memorial Museum, 2014. Web. 1 Dec. 2015.

4. "1939: Key Dates." *USHMM.org.* United States Holocaust Memorial Museum, 2014. Web. 1 Dec. 2015.

5. "WWI Casualty and Death Tables." *PBS.org.* Public Broadcasting Service, 2014. Web. 1 Dec. 2015.

6. "Warsaw." *USHMM.org.* United States Holocaust Memorial Museum, 2014. Web. 1 Dec. 2015.

7. "Threat of War." *AnneFrank.org.* Anne Frank House, 2014. Web. 1 Dec. 2015.

Chapter 4. A Year of Change

1. Anne Frank. *The Diary of a Young Girl: The Definitive Edition.* New York: Doubleday, 1995. Print. 1.

2. Ibid. 6.

3. "Amsterdam." *USHMM.org.* United States Holocaust Memorial Museum, 2014. Web. 1 Dec. 2015.

Chapter 5. The Secret Annex

1. Anne Frank. *The Diary of a Young Girl: The Definitive Edition.* New York: Doubleday, 1995. Print. 182.

2. Ibid. 26.

3. Ibid. 139.

4. Ibid. 44.

5. Ibid. 69.

6. Ibid. 81.

Chapter 6. In Hiding But Still Free

1. Anne Frank. *The Diary of a Young Girl: The Definitive Edition.* New York: Doubleday, 1995. Print. 133.

2. Ibid. 178.

3. Stewart Bentley. "The Dutch Resistance and the OSS." *CIA.gov.* Central Intelligence Agency, 14 Apr. 2007. Web. 1 Dec. 2015.

4. Anne Frank. *The Diary of a Young Girl: The Definitive Edition.* New York: Doubleday, 1995. Print. 251.

5. Ibid. 231.

6. "D-Day." *USHMM.org.* United States Holocaust Memorial Museum, 2014. Web. 1 Dec. 2015.

7. "The Netherlands." *USHMM.org.* United States Holocaust Memorial Museum, 2014. Web. 1 Dec. 2015.

Chapter 7. The Deadliest Journey

1. "Westerbork." *USHMM.org.* United States Holocaust Memorial Museum, 2014. Web. 1 Dec. 2015.

2. "Deportation: Westerbork Camp 1942–1944." *Auschwitz.nl.* Dutch Auschwitz Committee, n.d. Web. 1 Dec. 2015.

3. "To Camp Westerbork." *AnneFrank.org.* Anne Frank House, 2014. Web. 1 Dec. 2015.

SOURCE NOTES CONTINUED

4. "Auschwitz." *AnneFrankGuide.net*. Anne Frank House, 2014. Web. 1 Dec. 2015.

5. Ernst Schnabel. "A Tragedy Revealed: A Heroine's Last Days." *Life*. Time Inc., 1 Jan. 1958. *Google Book Search*, 1 Dec. 2015. 80.

6. "Kapos." *TheHolocaustExplained.org*. London Jewish Cultural Centre, 2014. Web. 1 Dec. 2015.

7. "Arrival at Camp Auschwitz." *AnneFrank.org*. Anne Frank House, 2014. Web. 29 Sept. 2014.

8. "Transport and Arrival." *TheHolocaustExplained.org*. London Jewish Cultural Centre, 2014. Web. 1 Dec. 2015.

9. "Tattoos and Numbers: The System of Identifying Prisoners at Auschwitz." *USHMM.org*. United States Holocaust Memorial Museum, 2014. Web. 1 Dec. 2015.

10. Matt Lebovic. "What Happened to Anne Frank after the Secret Annex?" *Times of Israel*. Times of Israel, 14 Sept. 2014. Web. 1 Dec. 2015.

11. "The Fate of the Women." *AnneFrank.org*. Anne Frank House, 2014. Web. 29 Sept. 2014. 84.

12. Ernst Schnabel. "A Tragedy Revealed: A Heroine's Last Days." *Life*. Time Inc., 1 Jan. 1958. *Google Book Search*, 1 Dec. 2015. 83.

13. "Bergen-Belsen." *USHMM.org*. United States Holocaust Memorial Museum, 18 Aug. 2015. Web. 1 Dec. 2015.

14. Matt Lebovic. "What Happened to Anne Frank after the Secret Annex?" *Times of Israel*. Times of Israel, 14 Sept. 2014. Web. 1 Dec. 2015.

Chapter 8. Liberated at Last

1. "Battle of the Bulge." *USHMM.org*. United States Holocaust Memorial Museum, 2014. Web. 1 Dec. 2015.

2. "Nazi Camps." *USHMM.org*. United States Holocaust Memorial Museum, 2014. Web. 1 Dec. 2015.

3. "Victims' Shoes." *USHMM.org*. United States Holocaust Memorial Museum, 2014. Web. 1 Dec. 2015.

4. Franciszek Piper. "The Topography of the Camp." *En.Auschwitz.org*. Auschwitz-Birkenau State Museum, 2005. Web. 1 Dec. 2015.

5. Ibid.

6. "Auschwitz." *USHMM.org*. United States Holocaust Memorial Museum, 2014. Web. 1 Dec. 2015.

7. “Back in Amsterdam.” *AnneFrank.org.* Anne Frank House, 2014. Web. 1 Dec. 2015.

8. Jennifer Chao. “Anne Frank’s Final Days Recalled—Dutch Woman Met Famed Author of Diary on the Train to Auschwitz.” *Seattle Times.* Seattle Times Network, 16 Mar. 1995. Web. 1 Dec. 2015.

9. Miep Gies. “A Futile Search For Survivors.” *Sun-Sentinel.com.* Sun Sentinel, 4 Jun. 1987. Web. 1 Dec. 2015.

10. “Diary of Anne Frank 65 Years in Print.” *AnneFrank.org.* Anne Frank House, 2014. Web. 1 Dec. 2015.

Chapter 9. Anne’s Legacy

1. “Anne Frank’s Diary Is Published.” *AnneFrank.org.* Anne Frank House, 2014. Web. 1 Dec. 2015.

2. Toni Jones. “Anne Frank’s Stepsister Eva Schloss on Living with the Legacy of the WWII Diarist.” *DailyMail.co.uk.* Associated Newspapers Ltd., 26 Apr. 2013. Web. 1 Dec. 2015.

3. “Reactions to ‘The Secret Annex.’” *AnneFrank.org.* Anne Frank House, 2014. Web. 1 Dec. 2015.

4. “After the Betrayal and After the War.” *MiepGies.nl.* Miep Gies: Her Own Story, 2014. Web. 1 Dec. 2015.

5. “Diary of Anne Frank 65 Years in Print.” *AnneFrank.org.* Anne Frank House, 2014. Web. 1 Dec. 2015.

6. “Publication in Many Languages.” *AnneFrankGuide.net.* Anne Frank House, 2014. Web. 1 Dec. 2015.

7. “Nelson Mandela on the Diary of Anne Frank.” *AnneFrank.org.* Anne Frank House, 2014. Web. 1 Dec. 2015.

8. Ibid.

9. “International Youth Centre.” *AnneFrank.org.* Anne Frank House, 2014. Web. 1 Dec. 2015.

10. Anne Frank. *The Diary of Anne Frank: The Revised Critical Edition.* New York: Doubleday, 2003. *Google Book Search,* 1 Dec. 2015. 623.

INDEX

ABOUT THE AUTHOR

Alexis Burling has written dozens of articles and books for young readers on a variety of topics, including current events and famous people, nutrition and fitness, careers and money management, and relationships and cooking. She is also a book critic with reviews of both adult and young adult books, author interviews, and other industry-related articles published in the *New York Times*, *Washington Post*, *Chicago Tribune*, and more. Burling remembers reading Anne Frank's diary for the first time in middle school. The experience inspired her to start keeping a journal of her own.